Wealth Zones

How to Locate Your Economic Zip Code

Jonathan Ferguson

Copyright © 2014 Jonathan Ferguson

ISBN-10: 1495494977

ISBN-13: 978-1495494970

In my forty years of ministry, I have met very few people like Jonathan Ferguson. I have often told him that his wisdom is beyond his years. Once reading Wealth Zones, you will understand why.

Wealth is a very sensitive issue and many have abused it for selfish gain. However, this book is filled with prophetic revelation that will make crooked paths straight and free you that you may be able to not only give cheerfully, but also be able to receive the abundance that God has stored up for you.

I can list many precious jewels that he presents to us, but when he states that money is a holy thing in the eyes of God, that really caught my attention and reminded me of how true that is.

This is a must read and a great investment into your life. Your Wealth Zone is waiting for you! Great job Jonathan! To God be the glory!

Jim DiPalma
Founder/Apostle/Author
World Overcomers Church / Encounter Church

Other Books by the Jonathan Ferguson Include:

Prophets 101
An Amazon #1 Hot New Release & Top 10 Best Seller

Experiencing God in the Supernatural
Newly Revised: Prophetic Acceleration

Learning the Language of God

Boot Camp Prayer & The Art of War

More Coming This Year (2014):

Conquering the Crossroads: 40-Day Devotional for Single Ladies
By Amanda Ferguson

Amanda's Story: Overcoming Molestation & Depression
By Amanda Ferguson

Claiming the World for Jesus: A Modern-Day Guide for Apostolic & Prophetic Evangelism
By Jonathan Ferguson

Contents

mammon works in order to hinder economic shifts and how to guard against it

- Understand how mammon deploys other agents such as depression, sickness and etc. in order to keep individuals in bondage and why these tactics will not succeed in your life

Chapter 3: Levels of Economic Empowerment 40

- Understand progression of provision, increase, and overflow
- Understand the power and purpose of provision
- Understand the difference between our budget and God's provision
- Examine the reality of Solomon's provisions in building the temple and embrace a concept of limitless resources
- Understand why there are different levels of economic empowerment

Chapter 4: Finding Your Wealth Zone 50

- Understand God's original plan for luxurious living
- Understand why the unbeliever at times can seem to be accessing more wealth than believers
- Understand how a believer has access to wealth that an unbeliever does not

because of the blessing
- Understand what a wealth zone is
- Learn how to find your wealth zone
- Learn two things that you can do in order to discern and not miss wealth transfers

- Learn what Pison represents
- Understand heaven's perspective of our money
- Understand why having a healthy work ethic is only half of what it takes to prosper in the Kingdom
- Understand the power and principles of tithing and sowing seed
- Understand pitfalls that are to be avoided for those who trust in their work ethic more than God's principles of tithing and sowing
- Understand the difference between working a job and working in the area of your purpose

- Learn what Gihon represents
- Understand what has more worth than money in the earth
- Understand that your hidden potential and God given gifts are designed to generate wealth as you cultivate them

- Observe the widow woman's encounter with Elisha, Learn from how she overcame financial crisis, and adjust your perspective of economic hardship

- Learn what the Tigris represents
- Learn how revelation can release supernatural wealth
- Learn the 3 Dimensions of financial harvest and how revelation can accelerate harvest
- Learn how you can see an accelerated harvest in your personal life

- Learn what the Euphrates river represents
- Understand God's commitment to fight for your finances and make the enemy repay you
- Learn how the prophetic anointing is connected to financial deliverance
- Learn of a wealth transfer that took place at the birth of Moses and what it represents
- Understand God's ability and prophetic promise to resurrect your finances

- Understand the economy and currency system of heaven
- Learn what it means to get paid by God and 3 ways to do so
- Receive a prayer of impartation and never go back to lack and poverty another day in your life

Chapter 1

Goodbye Mammon

Chapter Objectives:

- Begin your journey by understanding principles that are foundational in helping you embrace a biblical perspective of money
- Understand that money is not evil
- Learn two ways that the devil tries to deceive you concerning money
- Understand two misconceptions the devil wants you to have concerning money
- Begin to understand what mammon is
- Understand why you must deal with mammon aggressively in order to truly embrace wealth and prosperity
- Embrace the challenge and rewards of truly seeking the kingdom of God

Money has almost become a "curse word" in the context of religion. However, why would God Himself inform us that the silver and gold belonged to Him if money were evil (Haggai 2:8)? In fact, if the earth belongs to the Lord, why wouldn't the money in the earth be available to the people in the earth that likewise belong to the Lord (Psalm 24:1)? Why would God create a world that housed everything man would ever need, and in that include a supply of gold near the Garden of Eden if money were evil (Genesis 2:10-11)?

Why would the scriptures teach that money answers all things if money were evil (Ecclesiastes 10:19)? Why would the wealth of the wicked be handed over to the righteous if being broke were the righteous way to be (Proverbs 13:22; Ecclesiastes 2:26)? There are some questions that obviously need to be answered.

The truth of the matter is that the enemy desires to use every means possible in order to either convince people that God wants Christians broke, or to even discredit the integrity of Christian leaders in the area of money. It is nothing less than a demonic strategy to block the finances necessary to advance the Kingdom of God in the earth. However, I prophesy that there is an anointing being released as you read this book to break the back of poverty and call forth the resources necessary for you to fulfill God's plan for your life.

God Wants You Wealthy

Money is a holy thing in the eyes of

11

God. Therefore, when we are dealing with money, we are dealing with a spiritual matter. Make no mistake about it; God wants us wealthy. In fact, go ahead, take a moment, and say it out loud…. "God wants me wealthy." That's right, just take your time and say it again, if you'd like, because there is an anointing being released into the atmosphere around you every time you say it.

Nevertheless, if you have trouble saying and believing something that simple, this is definitely a book you would want to read over and over again. And on the contrary, if you enjoyed saying that God wants you wealthy, you believe in what you said, and maybe you're already experiencing it as well; this is still a book for you. No matter where you may find yourself in your walk with God, I'm convinced that you will be blessed as you read and maybe also compelled to purchase this book for others who may need it.

The Bottom Line

It is true that God wants us wealthy, but whether we desire the capacity to receive that wealth is totally up to us. Regardless to whatever you choose, you should know that God loves those who choose to be wealthy and those who do not to the same degree. It is not a sin to be rich and there is no such thing in the

Bible as a "vow to poverty".

In fact, it is time for all people, including religious leaders, who want to be broke to be broke by themselves and stop trying to make it a moral or spiritual standard for everyone else. The devil is a liar. The bible says that poverty brings destruction. In fact, we know, according to John 10:10, that it's the enemy that comes to destroy, but Jesus came to do the opposite and bring us life more abundantly.

Jesus Wants Us to Have a Talk About Money

I want you to understand that it is God who wants me to teach you about money in this book. I must make that very clear because many believe that it's impossible for an individual to deal with money and remain spiritual at the same time. Therefore, allow me to validate this once and for all.

I have been on multiple extended liquid-only fasts, including one that extended forty-seven days. I have had encounters with the Lord Jesus, angels, and various other prophetic experiences. I have even had outer-body visits into heaven; however, I insist that the manifest presence of Jesus is greater than any prophetic encounter that anyone could ever have.

13

I have seen cancer healed, tumors disappear, and I've witnessed other healings that have been clinically verified. God has used me in causing the paralyzed to walk and the deaf to hear. I have also seen countless saved and filled with the Holy Spirit with evidence of speaking with new tongues.

I believe in both preaching, and demonstrating the word that is preached with power. I'm very much into the supernatural and have written a best-selling book on the prophetic (*Prophets 101*). I've been there and gotten the t-shirt and I am yet hungry for more. However, in the midst of "all of my spirituality", the Lord spoke to me out of Luke 4:18 and said, "Son if you don't have *good news* for *broke people*, you are not anointed."

This is where the game changed for me. I realized that there are so many who experience a disconnect when it comes to **spirituality** and money. This just should not be, and this very issue is the reason why Jesus wants me to write to you about money.

Yes I said it; Jesus wants me to write to you about money because He wants you wealthy. And by now, if you still don't believe that—it's just too bad, but there is a reason that you still have not put the book down yet. You are still reading this book right now because in one of the hardest economic times in the history of the world, God wants you to understand His promise to you and your children concerning your money.

For this reason, I'm inviting you to boldly take this journey. Lay aside every preconceived notion and just give the Lord your undivided attention as you read. I promise your life will never be the same.

Refuse the Deception

One of the first of two things that I believe causes us not to maximize our economic potential is our perception of money. The second would be a misappropriation in the ways in which we handle money. The enemy often invests much effort in influencing these matters so that we do not truly benefit from one of the greatest resources that God has allocated to the earth in order for us to fulfill His purposes.

Furthermore, if there were two main misconceptions that the enemy uses in order to keep Christians stagnant financially, one would be to have us think that money is evil. The second would be to have us think that we must live in poverty in order to make it into heaven.

However, God never said that money is

evil; He only said that the love of money is the root or the cause of evil (1 Timothy 6:10). And Jesus never taught that it is hard for the rich to enter into heaven; He only said it's hard for those who put their trust in how rich they are to enter into heaven (See Mark 10:23-24).

The reason that the devil succeeds in perpetrating lies and causing many misconceptions concerning finances is simply because of a lack of knowledge. This is why I have decided to dedicate the first two chapters of this writing in dealing with some of primary misconceptions pertaining to your money and your relationship with God. Afterwards, we will deal with the both the power and transfer of wealth. We will examine the real issues that God has with money, how in fact God wants us to have money, and to what extent He has gone to ensure we never lack it.

This book will change the way you think about money whether you consider yourself a Christian or not. For this reason, I challenge you to read the entire book before coming to a conclusion about anything that is mentioned. You will find the reading to be both confrontational and empowering, therefore, don't be quick to get offended over something that you read, but rather first examine the whole matter.

However, I must warn you that similar to

the way that God used Jeremiah, I must tear some things down before I can build (Jeremiah 1:10). There are some mentalities about money that must be broken because they are strongholds that are hindering the wealth that God has for us. If you are up for the challenge, I can assure you that this book will increase your faith concerning finances like no other.

Prayer for Salvation

I want you to know that when I began writing this book I understood that it would attract people who are sure about their relationship with Jesus as well as people who are not. Therefore, before we go any further, if you are reading this and you are not sure that if you died right now that you would go to heaven, stop and pray the following prayer out loud with me:

Father, I thank You that You have set me up in this moment for me to come into relationship with You. Jesus, thank You for arresting my attention by Your Spirit and giving me the mind to even desire to pray this prayer. Jesus, I'm a sinner and I deserve to go to hell, but You took the punishment for my sin so that I wouldn't have to go there. I turn away from my sin now and I believe You will teach me how to live right from this day forward. Jesus, I believe You are the Son of God, and I believe that You have been raised from the dead after dying for

17

my sins. Thank You for saving me now. I trust in You for my life to be changed forever. Now fill me with Your Spirit and show me how to live for You more in Your name Jesus, Amen.

If you prayed that prayer, get in a good Bible believing church and let them know what happened to you. Let them help guide you in the process of your new walk with the Lord concerning the next steps you should take, and trust that God Himself is guiding you every step of the way. Feel free to also connect with my wife and I on social media via twitter, Facebook, instagram, and etc. And now back to this powerful teaching on money and wealth. Buckle your seat belt because this will be an awesome ride!

The Issue at Hand: The spirit of mammon

If we are going to understand the wealth that God has ordained for us to have and enjoy, we must be willing to expose and confront the reality that there is an evil spirit behind all of the world's problems in reference to money. It is in fact an evil that many unknowingly come into a business contract with in order to gain economically through various unethical means. This unclean spirit is called the spirit of mammon.

It is an evil entity that can influence an individual's perspective of money, an individual's bad decisions about money, and much more. Mammon keeps people in poverty and under economic oppression. And believe it or not, it is this spirit that doesn't want preachers and churches to be wealthy.

In fact, this spirit wants to control finances for the religious and non-religious alike. Whether people believe that there is such a spirit or not, it is at work behind the scenes and we must break its power if we are going to see wealth properly appropriated in the earth in the way that God originally intended.

Mammon & Love of Money

Jesus talks about mammon in Luke 16:9-13 and Matthew 6:24. It can be defined as wealth personified. It literally means money deified. In other words, this is a ruling spirit, power, and personality that invaded the culture and influenced the people's minds during the times in which Jesus lived in the earth.

With all of the perversions that were influencing the culture, Jesus puts the love of money at the center. James 4:1-3 continues in this revelation as James exposes the reasons for wars and violence among nations. Paul confirms this truth in 1 Timothy 6:10 as he

19

deals with the love of money.

Notice, I want to reiterate that in 1 Timothy 6:10, it's not money that is said to be evil, but rather the love of money being the root or the cause of the evil. Money is neutral in the text. Therefore, it of itself cannot necessarily sway an individual either way, good or evil, but it can reveal who they are.

In Matthew 6, Jesus was teaching that if we do not rid our lives of this spirit we would never truly experience the Kingdom of God. This is why there was such a radical type of initiation into the Kingdom that is introduced to the disciples of Jesus. For example, it is in Matthew 6 that Jesus told His disciples not to even think about how they were going to provide for themselves, but to rather seek His Kingdom first.

In others cases, Jesus instructed those who wished to follow Him to sell all they had and give to the poor. However, He didn't tell them that they would remain poor, but that they would receive one hundred fold more in both this lifetime and in the life to come (Mark 10:28-31).

Now could you imagine the shock value that the promise of Mark 10:28-31 had in people's lives? Jesus didn't say that they would receive a hundred times more, but a hundred fold more. This is significant because one hundred times more is just one times a hundred, but one hundred fold more is greater because a fold is multiplied by four and then that a hundred times over.

Jesus was saying, "I want to give you more than you can imagine, but I have to know that you can let it all go first. You have to show me that you can *have it* without *it having you.*"

This is why the spirit of mammon has to be dealt with head on and aggressively because of how subtle it is in its pursuit to enslave us. We will never have all that God desires for us financially until we deal with this evil spirit. Therefore, although there are countless revelations concerning finances that will empower you in this book, I must equally confront the very spirit that will attempt to hinder the manifestation of what you will learn.

Make no mistake about it; you will learn extensively about God's promises and power of wealth given to you. However, I must warn you again that this book is also designed to confront anything in you that's in agreement with the spirit of mammon. Therefore, proceed at your own caution. One thing I can guarantee is that if you allow the Lord to speak to you through these pages, you can get ready to say good-bye to poverty and good-bye to mammon.

Chapter 2

Money and Church

Chapter Objective:
- Understand the revelation of economics hidden in the story of Jesus multiplying the fish and the bread to feed the thousands
- Understand what an economic shift is
- Understand how economic shifts were customary in the lives of Jesus, the historical prophets, and the early church
- Understand why giving is key for you to experience similar economic shifts
- Understand how and why the spirit of mammon works in order to hinder economic shifts and how to guard against it
- Understand how mammon deploys other agents such as depression, sickness and etc. in order to keep individuals in bondage and why these tactics will not succeed in your life

The Miracle of Multiplication

In Mark 6:37 there is a story of how Jesus multiplied fish and bread in order to feed multiple thousands. However, many only talk about how the bread and fish multiplied and yet miss a powerful revelation concerning economics. Truth is, the revelation of the text does not only exist in how Jesus fed the multitude, but also in how much money it would have taken to feed them.

Mark 6:37 indicates that it would have taken at least "two hundred pennyworth" of bread in order to feed the multitude. The significance of this is that the particular amount would have been estimated at a year's worth of wages at that time according to research. Therefore, you have to understand that the disciples questioned Jesus about the budget not only because they knew that they could not feed the multitude, but also because they knew that there was no existing market at the time from which they could even purchase the necessary food.

The question in the text is evidence that the disciples of Jesus obviously understood the economic significance of the miracle that was needed in feeding the thousands. Just think about it. Could you imagine the market place at that time losing a year's worth of wages? This miracle was nothing short of an economic shift.

Economic Shifts

When I read Mark 6:37, there is no

question in mind concerning how the miracle ministry of Jesus literally shifted the economy much like the miracle ministries of Elijah, Moses, and other prominent prophets. In fact, the famous story of how Elijah commanded the rain was an economic move on his part. It was so powerful that it affected the economy of the entire world for 3 years, and I can show you how.

I explain this briefly in my book *Prophets 101*, but just in case you have not read it yet, you need to understand that the reason that the rain had so much effect on the economy is because of how the economy of that day was agriculturally based. In other words, most of what supplied the economy was land produced. The rain is then significant because it is necessary to the quality of the land.

Therefore when Elijah prophesied that there would be no rain we have to understand that in prophesying about the rain he simultaneously prophesied about the economy. No rain meant no harvest and no harvest meant no economy and because of it, the Bible says that there was a recession in the land until the day that Elijah said that it was time to rain again.

The truth is that there are always economic shifts when there is a move of God and God is always looking for the right people to steward over it (Ecclesiastes 5:9-10). In fact, the same power that heals and delivers is the same power that gets wealth according to Deuteronomy 8:18. It is the power of God that releases the blessing in our lives for the purposes of His covenant being established. Furthermore, the day has long been over for the Church to have a form of godliness and yet continue to deny God's power (2 Timothy 3:5).

Economic shifts are a part of the New Testament Christian reality and lifestyle, yesterday, today, and forever. The book of Acts clearly shows that when the Spirit of God is moving in a particular community, it is not an uncommon thing for finances to be redirected out of the hands of the wicked.

In Acts 16:16-19, Paul disrupted the economy of an entire city simply by casting a demon of divination out of a woman who was making money by giving psychic readings. A similar thing happened in Acts 19:22-27 when Paul began to preach against idolatry. These things took place because whenever God moves, financial channels that support demonic agendas begin to close.

Economics also begin to shift so that finances can be streamed in the proper direction. The church of Acts 4 is another great testimony of this reality. It was in Acts 4:33-37 that the church had great favor, and as a result there was no one that lacked anything because the finances were being properly distributed.

Could you imagine a culture where lack and poverty does not exist? Well, that is exactly how the culture of the early Church looked. And that is exactly the culture that the Church is returning to.

In Acts 4 there were even wealthy individuals who were selling their possessions so that they could have more money to give to the church. And eventually, because of how much money would come into the church, the apostles were able to begin redistributing the wealth.

Therefore, Acts 4 is very significant because, in our day, there are many that would be either nervous or irritated at even the thought of someone attempting to redistribute wealth, let alone the reality of it. However, you couldn't pay an individual enough not to participate in the type of culture that was being established in Acts 4 when they have a revelation of Kingdom economics.

The truth is that the initiation into this type of culture is giving. In fact, the attitudes and practices we have in our giving reveal the way we think about money. Therefore, the difference between an individual who is and is not living in a culture of blessing, increase, favor, and overflow is the way they choose to think about money.

The reason that the church of Acts 4 experienced such economic empowerment is because they were delivered from mammon and they understood that giving was key in experiencing the favor of God. Now don't misunderstand me, giving is by far not the only thing that this book will cover. However, it is necessary we lay a brief foundation in this area if we are truly going to conquer the spirit of mammon that comes to rob us of God's favor in our lives.

Spirit of Mammon in the Church

Many tense up when the Church deals with money because of the spirit of mammon. I want to reiterate that this takes place because mammon is literally a demon that wants to either keep people broke or keep them idolizing the money they do have. In reality, believers should be stewarding economics in the earth but won't until we understand the biblical truths of wealth.

Therefore, the Church should be both teaching about finances often and challenging individuals to practice the initial discipline that results in financial increase, which is giving. The conflict however is that when an individual is in bondage to mammon they feel as if giving to the church is a gimmick for the preacher to get money. When in reality it is an opportunity for the individual who gives to be blessed.

You can always tell what spirit has dominated an individual's mind by the way he/she responds when it is time to give in the offering. So many are very confused when it comes to this area in the Church. The proof of the confusion is that there are some that will spend hundreds and thousands of dollars shopping and then hesitate on a $20 offering.

Hosea the prophet said of this type of people that it is as if there are holes in their pockets. Even though they make money, they are not always able to enjoy it because they have built their own houses before they made sure that God's house was taken care of. In other words, they were investing in their personal lives in times when they should have been investing in the Kingdom of God.

In addition to the previous, there are others who will give, but they do not give out of the right motive. They give for their tax return benefits. Some actually give to get a better prophecy than every one else, or because they were emotionally hyped or manipulated to give. Both types of people have never learned what God thinks about their money and therefore do not know how to properly respond to God in their giving in a way that is pleasing to Him.

When we learn what God thinks about the way we handle His money and the way we give to His work, we would become excited about giving—we would be like those in Acts 4 who were selling things just to bring an offering to the apostles' feet. Could you imagine people going to the pawnshop and exchanging items for money just to make sure they had an offering when they came to church?

In fact, in the days of Moses, the offering that was received was too much to be kept (Exodus 36:5). Could you imagine the preacher having to tell the people to stop giving in the offering because there was too much coming in and not enough room to receive it? I prophesy that the day is returning in which people will give and receive in amounts that are overflowing and overwhelming.

Ananias and Sapphira

Most know the story of Ananias and his wife Sapphira in Acts 5 concerning how they died because they lied about their offering. However what many fail to realize is that it was the spirit of mammon in operation in the lives of Ananias and Sapphira. And much like what's portrayed in the story, it's this same spirit that often comes in seasons where God challenges us as believers to give financially in a sacrificial way. Therefore, there are a couple of things we should notice in what Peter said while correcting them that will help us not allow the spirit of mammon to deceive us when it comes to how the church deals with the money that we give.

The first thing many notice from the text is how Peter exposed that the couple did not merely lie to him, but rather to the Holy Ghost about their giving. However, when Ananias and Sapphira lied to Peter they didn't know that in actuality they were lying to the Holy Ghost. In other words, Peter was saying to them that the money they gave as an offering was not between them and himself, but between them and God.

When people hold back in their giving they are not holding it from the preacher, but they are in actuality holding it back from God. This is an awesome revelation because, I reiterate, the number one deception people have with their money and church is they think that the preacher is after their money. Thank God for giving Peter this awesome revelation that the real issue is that God looks at the way we give to the church and considers it as the way we give to Him.

The second thing that I noticed concerning how Peter dealt with Ananias and

Sapphira about their money was that when he questioned them, he asked them "was it not your own". In other words, if you don't want to give, then don't—it is not wrong to choose not to give something that the Lord is not requiring you to give. However, it is wrong to act is if you are giving something that you are not.

It is also wrong to know what God requires us to give, not give it, and yet come give whatever we want and act religious about it as if nothing is wrong. Or to act as if God is to receive whatever we give. Some even go as far to act as if they are doing the church a favor by giving. Let me explain.

There are many that feel as if they cannot afford to tithe. And there are others that want to give God whatever they want and think that it's acceptable. However, we must remember that Cain gave God what Cain wanted to give God, but Abel rather gave God what God wanted.

The revelation is that the same spirit that deceived Ananias is the same spirit that deceived Cain. And it is the same spirit that sits in churches and attempts to talk people out of giving of their finances in ways that the Lord both requires and is pleased. This is nothing short of mammon in operation.

You see, the last thing that Peter asked

Ananias and Sapphira was why they allowed the enemy to deceive them in their giving. Therefore, I want to propose that if a person is deceived in the way they give, it is because they are allowing a spirit of mammon to control their lives. We must get free of this if we are going to see the true blessing of God in our lives and I'm going to show you how as you continue to read.

I want to reiterate that the reason that God gives us wealth is so that we can establish his covenant in the earth. This is why we give sacrificially to the ministry. This is also why we should want the preacher blessed so that as he does the work of the ministry, he is not dealing with unnecessary issues and concerns.

After all, the preacher has enough devils already to deal with than to have to worry about finances. However, the enemy does not want the preacher free of financial worries and concerns that could distract his focus. Therefore, the Church must be ready to confront the spirit of mammon as it attempts to hinder the move of God.

In fact, this spirit of mammon is so against the move of God in the earth that it will often deploy other spirits and agents as allies in attempt to hinder God's plans. Let's take a brief moment in conclusion of this chapter to look at how mammon will often partner with religion, politics, depressions and even sickness in attempt to hinder the Church.

Mammon and Sickness

This spirit of mammon so attempts to hinder the move of God that it has literally influenced various individuals to have a mentality in which they actually don't want to be healed because they want to keep their disability check. Others feel that as long as they have money and can pay for a cure that they don't really need God's healing power. However, there are others that love God and at times this spirit even attacks their lives in the form of sickness for no other reason but to deplete their financial resources.

This is what happened with the woman who had the issue of blood. The scriptures say that she had spent all her money, and still couldn't find a cure, which is what led her to the hem of Jesus' garment. I am prophesying that there are going to be such economic shifts that it will once again bring everyone back to the feet of Jesus. I prophesy an economy that will open to those who carry the healing power of God in their ministries. That in every way your ministry has been hindered due to finances, God now releases the resources you need in order to take God's healing power to the world.

Mammon, Religion, and Politics

Another way that the spirit of mammon tries to hinder the move of God is through religion and politics. The story of how Mary of Bethany poured costly oil on the feet of Jesus is a great example of this. In fact, the response of the religious group surrounding Jesus when she poured the perfume and costly oils on His feet exposes how this spirit was in operation. It is also a great example of how many miss the point when it comes to money if they are bound by mammon.

In John 12:3 when the oil was poured on the feet of Jesus, it offended the bystanders because of the deception that was in their hearts. However, the excuse they used for being offended is that instead of Mary pouring the perfume on the feet of Jesus, the perfume could have been sold and the money from it given to the poor. It sounds morally and politically correct. The only problem is, it was a cover for their greed and their alliance with the spirit of mammon. They were obviously just as deceived as Ananias and Sapphira were in Acts 5.

The deception is seen in Mary of Bethany's story in how the bystanders subtly challenged both the motive of what she gave and also the fact that Jesus is the one who received of what she gave. With the aforementioned scenario in mind, there is no coincidence that there is now a big controversy over how ministry money is spent. The reason is because the enemy desires to create a suspicion that is rooted in envy within the hearts of people, ultimately causing them to discredit the necessity of giving financially into the work of the Lord.

I'm not implying that there be no accountability concerning Church finances, but I am exposing the reality that although there are integral preachers who do right with money, there are yet also individuals who don't want to see the preacher blessed. In fact, there comes a level in your giving where you really don't tap into real wealth until you start giving beyond the ministry and directly into the man or the woman of God with a desire to see them blessed even in their personal lives.

Nevertheless, in John 12:7-8, I love how Jesus challenged the spirit of mammon that was operating in the minds of the religious leaders. He basically informed them that there would always be opportunity to give to the poor, but there are some people that discern times in which they should give that are once-in-a-lifetime. This means, in part, that there are times when things should be given for no other reason but to bless the man or woman of God, in response to all of the spiritual things that have been received of the giver from the preacher, which is what the spirit of mammon does not want the Church to embrace.

The revelation of the text is that there are some people that only give to a cause, and that's good, but there are some people who discern once-in-a-lifetime opportunities to give in ways that dramatically alter both their spiritual and financial futures. For example, in Acts 10:1-4, there was a Centurion, of the Italian regiment, who had given so much that it came up as a memorial before God. This means that God forever remembers his offering. The same was said of Mary in John 12, in that she is remembered wherever the gospel is preached forever.

Therefore, we must be careful that we do not allow mammon to deceive us out of the favor of God. It is a very important thing to be mindful of this because there are many that unknowingly make inner vows with a spirit of poverty concerning how much they will never give to the Church. There are also many that pay dues to be in a denomination or to be apart of a ministerial fellowship. Or they give to charities for political reasons, but they have no memorial before God.

There are even those who give to be seen or give in order to connect with a famous preacher, yet they have no memorial before

God. There are preachers that know gimmicks of how to get people to give their money, and after the people give they still have no memorial before God. There are even false prophets that give the people all kinds of false prophecies that emotionally move the people to give, and yet there is no real reward to be obtained in it.

All of this is the spirit of mammon robbing people of their inheritance. However, when God remembers your offering, it is because you learn what pleases Him in the way you both handle your finances and give in obedience to Him. The truth of the matter is that it doesn't matter who you are not connected to, what denomination that does not endorse your ministry, or what prophecy you do not receive—as long as God honors your giving. This is why we can't afford to be religious or political concerning the reasons that we give.

It does not even matter what the preacher is doing with the money. Let God handle the preachers that are handling the money wrong, and you just make sure you are handling your money right. In the end you will discover that if you apply the principles of God's word in the way you handle your finances and obey in your giving, the blessing of God will be unstoppable in your life.

Mammon and Depression

The last demonic agent that mammon deploys in order to keep individuals in bondage that I would like to expose is depression. However, you will only understand this reality as you contemplate for a moment and realize that what most charismatic believers consider as an "attack from the devil", is often in reference to a struggle in their finances. In fact, most have not encountered any high level spiritual warfare because the enemy knows that if he can keep an individual depressed about money, he can pretty much take the fight out of them.

The same was true for the widow woman who baked the cake for the prophet Elijah in 1 Kings 17. She had become so depressed because of the economy that she was ready to give up and die. The story reveals how there are people that so struggle in their finances that they don't know how they are going to make it from one day to another. They don't know what they are going to eat, how they will pay their bills, or how they will provide for their children.

Many are in fact depressed about their financial situations that have caused them to live day by day, struggling to produce just "enough to get by". Thank God however that there is good news in the story of Elijah and the widow woman. And the good news is that God was not interested in just helping the widow woman get "enough to get by". In fact, by the time Elijah had finished with the widow, she not only had enough to bake a cake for the prophet, but she had enough to start a whole baking industry.

And on the basis of 1 Kings 17, I prophesy that the same type of prophetic anointing released into the widow's life through Elijah, to take that which was little and make it into much, is being released into your life. I'm decreeing that every depression that has been in your life concerning finances is leaving you now. I prophesy that as you continue and finish reading this book, God is about to increase you more financially than what you are expecting for. When He gets finished, you will have enough to take care of you, your children, and somebody else. You will be blessed and you will become a blessing in Jesus name. Amen.

Chapter 3

Levels of Economic Empowerment

Chapter Objectives:
- Understand the progression of provision, increase, and overflow
- Understand the power and purpose of provision
- Understand the difference between our budget and God's provision
- Examine the reality of Solomon's provisions in building the temple and embrace a concept of limitless resources
- Understand why there are different levels of economic empowerment

I want to gradually change the tone of my writing a bit and now begin to deal with economic empowerment. In fact, I believe that the more we understand various levels of economic empowerment, the better we can resist the spirit of mammon in our lives and be prepared for what God wants to do in our finances.

However, in order to understand this empowerment we must understand provision. Along with that, we should understand there are three different stages of how God's provision in our lives progresses as follows:

1) Provision
2) Increase
3) Abundance and Overflow

We need to know what level we are living on financially and how to increase that level. Understanding the nature and the progression of God's provision in our lives will help us do just that. The sobering truth in this revelation is that before we can go to the next level in our finances; we must master the one we are on.

Also, we must discern when God is taking us to the next level financially so that we can cooperate with that and be sure it manifests. I want to take this chapter and lay a strong foundation concerning the provision of God and explain how there are many levels of economic empowerment associated. After this I will take the next chapter and explain the progression of economic empowerment.

PROVISION

The word provision is made up of two

words. The primary word is "vision" defined in the Hebraic as redemptive revelation. The prefix is "pro" meaning "for" and together the word provision literally means "for the vision". Wherever there is vision, there is provision and anything below provision is poverty.

Philippians 4:19 provides us insight into how provision operates as scriptures speak of our needs being supplied according to the riches that are in the glory. I want to expound on this text because many only focus on the need being met when in actuality we should first understand that there are riches in glory. In other words, there is a heavenly budget to allocate resources for the vision God has given you.

Next, we should understand that God will supply all of our needs *ACCORDING TO* the riches that are stored up in glory. In other words, our provision is not according to our salary, but according to heaven's endless resources. The revelation is that God does not provide for us based on our budget, but based on the vision and purpose He has given us to pursue.

We will look at this scripture more in depth later in this chapter, but for now we need to understand that no vision equals no supply. Little vision equals little supply. More vision equals more supply. And finally, unlimited vision equals unlimited supply.

In fact, Solomon's budget for building the temple is a great example of the power of God's provision in our lives. The reason is that because his provisions were in proportion to the vision and instructions he had been given to build the temple. In other words, everything that was required in order for Solomon to build was provided for. Simply put, Solomon had vision, was given instruction, and the result was that his provisions were too much to be counted.

We've heard it said, "if its God's will, He will pay the bills", which is definitely something we can see demonstrated in the life of Solomon. In fact, in addition to the instructions for building the tabernacle, the scripture also interestingly gives insight concerning the details of the project's budget. Let's look at this in order to expand our minds concerning God's endless resource and mission to fund the life and assignment that He has called us to complete.

Solomon's Provisions

One of the resources that Solomon used in building the temple according to 2 Chronicles 3:8-9, included 600 talents of gold. This is significant in that out of the many provisions for the temple, this one provision put the temple value immediately into hundreds of billions. Let me show you how.

In the year of 2009, which is the year that God began dealing with me about this subject, the price of gold was $900 per ounce. This is important because it requires 16 ounces to make a pound, and 75 pounds to make one talent. If we calculate the price of gold and weight of 600 talents, it would put us at approximately 100 billion.

However the price of gold is not the same as it was in 2009. In fact, the price of gold is almost tripled in the U.S. being worth almost $1700 per ounce. This means that Solomon's budget for gold alone would have been worth over 300 billion today. And this was not even Solomon's complete budget. Better yet, it was not even close to 50% of the budget.

How Much is Your Vision Worth?

Apple Inc., one of the leading companies of our time, is worth over 900 billion, yet Apple Inc. is not even close to 10% of Solomon's temple worth. The scripture says the silver in Solomon's kingdom was worthless. This does not mean that it had no value, but that the value was beyond being calculated.

Scriptures also say of Solomon's provisions in 2 Chronicles 4:18, that the weight of brass could not be found out. This means that his budget was off the charts. But the real thing that you should consider is how much your vision is worth. Could it be that the vision and purpose God has planned for your life is worth more than hundreds of billions?

What I want you to understand is that in God's provision for you, your budget is not based on what you have and what you can afford. In the kingdom of God, there is no such thing as a waste of money or "too expensive". In fact, Psalm 144:13 teaches that your garners and storages are full and there is nothing that is unaffordable to you. You just have to learn how to tap into your heavenly account and get into your wealth zone.

The only thing that is too expensive for anyone—who is born again believer—is the thing that's beyond our management and vision. This is what I mean by levels of economic empowerment. It is very simple to understand. And the truth is that your level of economic empowerment is your level of provision, and your level of vision and level of money management will determine your level of provision.

Everyone doesn't live in the same level of economic empowerment because everyone is not allocated the same provisions. Everyone is not allocated the same provisions because everyone does not have the same level of vision. This means that those of you who believe for God to bring you into financial increase need to ask yourself the following questions:

What is it that God has called you to do? What are the visions and plans that God has placed in your heart? And lastly, how much do you think it is worth to God to make sure it is established in the earth?

There are many levels of provision that people are either experiencing or not experiencing. The truth is, although we have learned how the supply of God is beyond comprehension and beyond our ability to budget, there are yet many who never experience His abundance. There is a reason for this. People don't lack provision because there is not a supply, but because they are yet to have a proper vision of their money, and also an understanding of what God desires and is capable of manifesting in their lives.

Introduction to Progressing in Economic Empowerment

As I have fore-mentioned, the basis of economic empowerment is provision. Once we understand that, we should then understand that there is a process in the economic power of provision. Lastly, understanding the progression of economic empowerment is understanding that no matter what level we are on financially, God wants to increase us until we are overflowing abundantly.

We have learned that there are different levels of provision that people experience, which represents different levels of economic empowerment. We have also learned that there is a way to increase the level of provision we are experiencing from which I have named the stages of economic empowerment as follows: provision, increase, and overflow.

The first step into economic empowerment is allowing God to bring us out of poverty. This is provision at its basics. The release of its power is in knowing that your needs are always going to be taken care of.

There are however different levels of provision that we can access based on the way we manage what we have and the way we allow God to expand our life's vision. The progression of this economic empowerment is the process of how God progressively continues to increase the levels of provision that we experience. Once we tap into provision, God wants to keep "increasing" our "provision" until we find ourselves in the "overflow".

Therefore, in conclusion of this chapter, I want to briefly expound on this progression of economic empowerment as a foundation to understanding the various wealth that I will be begin explaining in the following chapter. The progression is as follows:

INCREASE is when God graduates you to the next level of provision or when He causes you to experience random releases of more than enough. When these random increases come, we should understand that they are either for our enjoyment, our savings, or they are our seed to be planted in hopes of an even greater increase. It is at this point that we are expected to discern which is which. In fact, God can trust us in this place of decision because the way we think about and spend our money has matured or else the increase would have never come in the first place.

OVERFLOW is when you can pay for your stuff and somebody else's also. In overflow, you become a distribution center. Many are yet to tap into the level of abundance and overflow. However, Philippians 4:19 still holds true that there are riches in glory.

There is supernatural money that can be released just as how when the disciples needed money to pay taxes, there was gold that was found supernaturally in the mouth of a fish (Matthew 17:27). In fact, I reiterate that the revelation in Philippians 4:19 is not just that God meets the need, but that He does so ACCORDING to a supply of riches in Glory. In other words, the supply you are about to pull from is greater than the need that is about to be met. And it is because He meets the need according to a greater supply that, after the need is met, there will be an overflow that remains. If you do not believe me, just ask the multitudes that were fed the fish and the loaves in Mark 6.

If you want to increase your level of economic empowerment, you have to increase the level of your provision. If you want to increase the level of your provision, you have to increase your vision. When your vision increases, it will be evident in both the way you think about money and the way you spend it.

Chapter 4

Finding Your Wealth Zone

Chapter Objectives:
- Understand God's original plan for luxurious living
- Understand why the unbeliever at times can seem to be accessing more wealth than believers
- Understand how a believer has access to wealth that an unbeliever does not because of the blessing
- Understand what a wealth zone is
- Learn how to find your wealth zone
- Learn two things that you can do in order to discern and not miss wealth transfers

God's Financial Plan

The intent of God to bless us can be traced all the way back to when God planted the Garden of Eden in Genesis 2:7. In fact, the word Eden literally means "a place in God", and it also means luxurious living—just to name a few. There are other definitions, but the revelation I want you to get from this is that God is the author of luxury.

It was in Eden that the blessing was first given. In fact, God never intended that we work hard to be blessed. It was only after the curse that we began producing by our hard labor and sweat. But thanks to God, we can now all live under the blessing again instead of the curse because of what Jesus accomplished on the cross (Galatians 3:13).

God has always wanted us to be blessed and always will want us to be blessed...and that settles it. A great confirmation of this reality can be found in Genesis 2:11. It is there that the scripture teaches that one of Eden's rivers flowed into a place where there was gold.

Obviously, God had money in mind at the beginning, or why else would there be a need for gold? The truth is that before God created us, He had already made provisions for everything thing we would ever need. Therefore, it is a smack in God's face to teach that we are called to just barely make it in life. The devil is a liar.

Even after Adam and Eve sinned, the Bible says that man was kicked out of the garden, but it does not say that they were kicked out of Eden. In fact, the first man that left Eden was Cain, not Adam, but people who don't really read their Bibles do not know this. However, in order to understand this we have to understand that the garden was not called Eden, but rather the garden was a place that was located in Eden.

Let me make this plain. The relevance of being kicked out of the garden as opposed to being kicked out of Eden is God basically saying to mankind, "even though you messed up, this money thing is still going to be an important factor in your life." Therefore, when God kicked Adam and Eve out of the garden, He blocked the tree of life, and they no longer had access into certain places within Eden.

In blocking the tree of life, God was basically saying, "I can't let you live forever in this state of sin, but I won't kick you out of Eden." It was almost as if God was saying, "There is still some luxury I'm going to let you have while you are still here in the earth, but because of the curse you are going to have to work hard to see it."

It is for this reason that there are sinners that seem to be more blessed than some Christians. The truth is that sinners are not more blessed than Christians. However, they do know how to work their system of economics. And when you learn how to work your system, even the curse can't stop you from being blessed.

God, in His mercy, has made things where—whether we are sinners or saved—we would still be able to produce. However, because of the curse, there will just be a lot of hard work involved, unless you know how to tap into the blessing. But apart from the blessing, the sinner and saved alike have equal opportunity in living a luxurious life, although such is not a pursuit of the believer.

This is what the scripture means that God rains on the just and the unjust. It means that although the unjust are not saved, God still causes the principles that they live by to produce wealth on their behalf. And if it were not for God, even the atheist wouldn't be able to produce any wealth. The issue that rises for me is that if a sinner can produce wealth under the curse, how much more should a Christian under the blessing?

Wealth Zones

The revelation of the wealth zones is found in that there was a river that flowed *OUT* from the garden, and from there it parted into four heads or streams. In other words there was only *ONE* source, but yet many resources. I believe that this is prophetically symbolic of how God wants us all economically empowered, but He just doesn't want us to forget who and what our real source is.

It is amazing to me that even after the grounds were cursed, there were still four streams of luxury (Eden) accessible to man. In fact, I believe these rivers represent financial streams, or what I like to call *Wealth* Zones, simply because of the location and nature of where the streams led. You will understand this truth more and more as you continue to read.

However, the more obvious truth is that although man had been kicked out of the garden, they were still connected to the source. They literally had access to multiple streams of income, although they had to work hard for it. Therefore, if God is not intimidated for sinners to be financially empowered, why are we as Christians sometimes intimidated to receive the even greater economic empowerment that comes in the blessing?

Getting into your Wealth Zone

I believe it is prophetically significant that scripture emphasizes the location of the garden in Genesis 2:7, and in that it was located to the east of Eden. It is significant because there is correlation of wealth and location. Let me explain.

Deuteronomy 8:18 talks about power to get wealth. However, in order to understand the depths of Deuteronomy 8:18, we must understand that wealth and money are different.

Money is in fact currency, but wealth is a commodity. Furthermore, in order to have currency there must first be an exchange of a commodity. Therefore, wealth is greater than money because it gives currency its value.

The truth is that you can have money and not be wealthy. If you don't believe that, just ask the people who lost millions of dollars when the stocks fell in 2008. However, it is not possible to be wealthy and not have money.

When you possess wealth, the market can crash and it not affect you because you are not just dealing with the currency, but you are supplying the commodity. In fact, those who possess wealth understand that as long as you have real wealth, you will always be able to make an exchange for currency no matter how bad the economy. Therefore, when you as a believer understand that you posses wealth within you, you don't get nervous when your "money acts funny" because you understand that the currency is designed to follow the wealth that is inside of you.

However, the primary thing we should

understand about wealth in order to understand the prophetic implication of Genesis 2:7 is that the wealthiest commodities are found in natural resources and land. This means that natural resource is where the real wealth is because there is always a demand for it to be exchanged for currency. This is important because one thing that is consistent when dealing with natural resources and commodities is that they are geographical. This means that wealth is always found in a particular place or location.

In fact, there are certain places that God created with certain valuable natural resources already in the land. For example, oil is more prominent in the Middle East, yet gold can be found in places where oil cannot. America is the land of coal, yet diamonds and other precious stones are found in Africa. As it is in the natural, so it is in the spirit. You must know your economic zip code. Selah.

There is a place that has your money. And the good news is that if you are not in the place you would like to be financially, all you have to do is change *WEALTH ZONES*. The Lord spoke to me years ago and said "Son there is no amount of gold or wealth that has ever left the earth".

This means that a famine or recession doesn't remove the wealth, it only shifts the wealth zone. In fact, the reason that money doesn't ever leave the earth is because heaven doesn't need it and hell can't have it. Therefore, whenever economic crisis comes, it only means that the wealth of the wicked is being transferred into the lives of the righteous.

Back to Eden

Eden was a place in the presence of God as we have previously mentioned, and to this day it is a fact that man cannot find the Garden of Eden. There can be many reasons for this, but the Holy Ghost gave me a revelation on this. He told me that we don't need to find in the natural what righteousness can find for us in the spiritual. However, this only makes sense if you understand that the word righteousness literally means to be in right standing or in the right "place" with God.

In other words, it does not matter if we cannot find the Garden of Eden—as long as we can access what was available in Eden through righteousness. Therefore, Eden can almost be considered as a type and shadow of the results of righteousness. In other words, righteousness becomes our Eden—our luxury, and our place of wealth—which is why if we will just get in the right place with God, it changes our economic zip code.

57

Discerning the Transfer

The previous revelation of Eden is an example of how we can often be looking for God to release things in our lives that we are not properly positioned to receive. This means that we often miss the move of God because we are not in the zone that He is moving in. The testimony of Israel's transition out of Egypt is another great example of this truth. I will briefly expound, but for more explanation on this you can read my book *Boot Camp Prayer & The Art of War*.

But when Israel was praying for deliverance out of the bondage of Egypt, an interesting thing took place. Although they were praying in Egypt, God sent the answer in the land of Midian; where Moses was. They were in one place, yet God sent the answer to another place. I believe this is prophetic of what we just learned of righteousness. And the truth is that sometimes we can be looking for God in one way and He comes in another.

Even the way in which God transferred the wealth of Egypt into Israel's hands is similar to this truth. For example, did you know that by the time Israel had made it to the "promised" land of Canaan, the wealth had already been transferred? In fact, Israel actually experienced the wealth prior to even entering the wilderness.

This means that just because you may be in a financial wilderness does not mean that there has not already been a wealth transfer. Therefore, we can't look at our circumstances around us and let that determine whether we are going to believe God for the wealth that He has already placed within us.

We are not called to analyze our wildness but we are called to transform it into a paradise. If we consider the wilderness in this season, we will be in danger dying in it just as the children of Israel did. They were so focused on the place they wanted God to take them that they overlooked the blessing of the place they were already in. However, the truth was that God had already transferred wealth in their lives.

Likewise, in our lives, the wealth transfer is not something that God is about to do, but something that is already taking place. However, in order to discern this we must do two things. The first thing we must do is to understand how this wealth transfer looks, and the second thing we must do is position ourselves to partake of it.

The good news is that the wealth that belongs to us is literally defined in the four rivers that flowed from Eden, which makes it easy for us to understand how God transfers wealth into our lives, as we understand what the four rivers represent. Therefore, throughout the remaining chapters, I want to define the four rivers that flowed out of the Garden of Eden as representing various wealth zones that we can tap into.

So I must warn you that you are in for a treat. The remaining chapters of this book are guaranteed to increase your expectation concerning your finances. And by the time you are done with this book, you would have learned principles of how to tap into God's financial flow for your life and you will find your wealth zone.

Chapter 5

Wealth Zone One-Pison

Chapter Objectives:

- Learn what Pison represents
- Understand heaven's perspective of our money
- Understand why having a healthy work ethic is only half of what it takes to prosper in the Kingdom
- Understand the power and principles of tithing and sowing seed
- Understand pitfalls that are to be avoided for those who trust in their work ethic more than God's principles of tithing and sowing
- Understand the difference between working a job and working in the area of your purpose

The first wealth zone that I want to deal with is called Pison. It is one of four rivers that flowed out of Eden and it literally means "to grow fat" or "to increase". The significance of this wealth zone is found in Genesis 2:11 as it talks about how this river flowed into a place where there is gold.

It's not a coincidence that there is an emphasis around the gold. And if we are going to understand the first wealth zone, we have to understand the significance of gold, which is currency. Therefore, in order to understand the revelation of the first wealth zone, we must examine some of the basic concepts of financial acumen and also heaven's perspective of money.

The initial concept of financial acumen is quite simple. It says that if we will work and make the proper investments God will increase us and cause our money to grow fat (Pison). It's, however, the next revelation concerning this wealth zone that many are yet to understand because it deals with how heaven looks at our money in context of the way we give. With that in mind, I must cover principles concerning giving that I strongly advise you to pay close attention to.

Understanding Our Money & Why Giving It is the Best Way to Increase It

We must understand spiritually that when heaven looks at our money, it sees it as either seed or bread according to 2 Cor. 9:10. In fact, if we look at 2 Corinthians 9:10 more closely, we will discover that the scripture is referencing how believers give to the Church out of their earned provisions in order to distinguish between their bread and their seed. So basically, your bread is your provision that you have worked to earn. And your seed consists of the investments you make into God's Kingdom, or in other words, the money you give into the work of the ministry that results in the increase of your provisions.

If you do not work, you do not eat. But if you work and do not sow seed, you cannot increase. In fact, even after you sow, you must yet work the ground that you have sown into in order to see the harvest.

Therefore, when dealing with money, we should understand that having a healthy work ethic and understanding the power of sowing seed is equally important. And most importantly of all, we should understand that the greatest investment we could ever make is the way we sow into the Kingdom of God. And this is where things get complicated for many.

Reason being is because although there are many that understand the importance of having a healthy work ethic, there are many who are yet to understand the significance of sowing. In fact, it is very difficult for some people to understand why giving our money to the Church is the greatest investment we could ever make. And I am convinced that they lack this revelation either because they either worship their money or they have never had to give their way out of poverty.

However, the reason that giving to the work of God is the greatest investment is because God will always guarantee that your return is over and above what you give. There is no other investment that can guarantee such a return. And those who have lost investments in stocks are a testimony to that reality.

Truth is, having a healthy work ethic alone is only one of the revelations needed in order to achieve maximum financial success. In fact, many have made small strides in attempt to get ahead in life while others have struggled to make ends meet simply because they were yet to realize how the principles of sowing and reaping were missing out of their equation. If we ever realize that while Adam worked in the garden of luxury (Eden), the only thing that he really had working for him was his seed, half of our problems would be solved.

Likewise, the only thing we have working for us that guarantees an economic return is our seed. We can work until we are blue in the face, but until we understand and apply the laws of sowing and reaping, we are missing out on the real wealth. In fact, everything we do in life is like a seed or an investment that will bring a harvest and a return in our lives (Galatians 6:7-8). Furthermore, the bible also says that every seed produces according to its own kind (Genesis 1:11-12).

That means if we sow time, we get time. If we sow an apple seed, we get an apple tree. So likewise, if we sow money, we will reap money. Therefore, if we are going to live at Pison, we have to embrace both the work we are called to do and the seed we are called to sow.

The Power of Sowing Seed

We must come to a place in our lives in which we understand that, at times, our work is the means for provision while, at other times, our work is a means for us to attain a seed. In other words, there are times when what you think is your bread becomes your seed. And if you properly invest your seed, great increase will follow.

In fact, if what we are working to produce is not amounting to what we need, our bread then becomes our seed. This means that there is a radical type of giving anointing that can come on our lives in which we can literally sow our way out of poverty. It means we can literally give our way into increase and abundance.

The widow woman in 1 Kings 17 is a great example of this in how she baked her very last meal and gave it to the prophet Elijah to eat in a middle of famine. She thought she was giving her bread away, but God received the meal that she baked for the prophet as a seed and because of it, she never lacked again.

It is hard for many to understand this type of giving, but Ecclesiastes 11:1-7 talks about it when it encourages us to cast our bread on many waters in the context of sowing and reaping. In fact, 1 Kings 17, Ecclesiastes 11, and many other scriptures are great examples concerning how God often ordains radical giving in order to bail individuals out of extreme poverty. It is only as we understand this reality and participate in it that we can access the wealth zone called Pison.

Many miss the blessing of entering into this type of place with God when it comes to giving because they feel as if they are giving away their hard earned money. On the contrary, God wants to bless them beyond what they can imagine as they learn to make the necessary investments a priority. In fact, the book of Proverbs teaches how giving is in actuality lending to the Lord (Proverbs 19:17).

This is significant because when the text

speaks about lending to the Lord, it doesn't mean that the Lord needs our money, but it means that heaven treats what we give as a loan, and therefore, God pays it with interest. This is why we have heard the saying that "we cannot out-give God". The truth of the matter is that God will always give back to us more than what we have given out into His purposes.

My wife and I have literally lived this even prior to us being married. As of March 7, 2014 we have been married just two years and not too long before then discovered that we both had sown our very 1st thousand-dollar seed in the year of 2008, which was the very year prior to us meeting on March 7, 2009. And what is even more significant is that we both were the very first individuals in our family to ever give on the thousand-dollar level.

Therefore, I want to briefly focus on the power of the thousand-dollar seed from my personal experience, but certainly not to imply that whatever seed you may sow is not just as significant, even if its only one dollar or less. Ultimately, the truth is that whenever and whatever you give, even if it's not a thousand-dollar seed, if it's the best you have to give, then that's all that matters. However, the following portion of testimony is simply what I felt prompted by the Lord to share as evidence to what extent that I personally practice and have proven the truths written in this book.

Our Testimony

When my wife and I reflect back, we can recognize the hand of God in connecting two individuals who decided to break out of the systemic poverty in our bloodlines. And the crazy faith about our history of giving is that, prior to our marriage, we both had sown thousand-dollar seeds into the ground of the kingdom at times when people around us thought it did not make sense. For example, when I sowed my first thousand-dollar seed, I was without a car and was living with someone that had taken me in and given me a place to stay. I even remember sowing a thousand-dollar seed on my birthday, which is in September, and followed up with another during the Christmas season of the same year.

I remember my wife sowing a thousand dollar seed in 2010, about 2 years prior to us being married, and almost immediately afterward her car had broken down leaving her carless until she met the owner of a car lot sitting in the first class section of a flight she was working. The owner gave her his business card after being impressed with her service and let her know that if she ever wanted a new car to contact him. When it was all said and done, she drove off the car lot in the car she wanted, and actually owned the car for weeks before actually signing the papers.

The point is that people just did not understand the faith that God had put in us to give our way into the place in which we wanted to go financially. However, for us, it didn't make sense to try and live off of what we had. In fact, Proverbs 11:24 teaches that there is one that withholds what is in his hand and it leads him into poverty. The same verse also says that there is one who disperses his substance and it causes him to increase although it does not make sense (Proverbs 11:24).

It did not make sense how my wife and I would give on such a large level when we didn't even have a consistent income. And yet there are people who work "nine to five" and struggle with giving a hundred dollar seed. However, some things will never make sense; they will only make faith.

When my wife and I sowed, we obviously needed the money and there were obviously other things we could have spent the money on, but we gave it instead. Prior to our marriage we both already had a history of literally saving up thousand-dollar lump sums and sowing them as seeds into the Kingdom of God on multiple occasions. And we literally kept sowing the thousand-dollar seed out of our need until we reached the place where we could sow it out of our overflow.

This is why no one can tell me that tithing, sowing, and reaping is not biblical and that it's a gimmick for preachers to get money because it's all I had and it's all any believer will ever have as a sure way to financial overflow. I had to learn this principle because nothing else worked for me. And even when I began to sow my seeds, the results did not come in over night. I had to make sowing a lifestyle, which is why I want to briefly cover some basic truths we should understand about sowing and reaping before we proceed.

Basic Laws of Sowing and Reaping

Let's take a moment to examine an often hidden truth in Genesis 8:22 concerning seedtime and harvest. And please be sure that we will cover some more advanced principles of seedtime and harvest in a later chapter, but for now I want to cover a basic principle that I believe will remove any fear there may be in your heart concerning giving your money into the Kingdom of God.

For years I have read Genesis 8:22 and understood sowing and reaping to be God's system of economic empowerment. However, I recently noticed something in the text that sealed a greater faith in my heart when I not only paid attention to the seedtime and harvest portion of the text, but rather the "as long as the earth remains" portion of the text. The Lord spoke to me from the text and said: *When you sow, I am obligated to bless you until the day that Jesus returns and even for as long as the earth exists.*

This is very significant because the text is assuring us that no matter what happens in the world's economy, those who sow are guaranteed economic safety, financial preservation, and irreversible increase. This means that our financial system will never crash. It also means that streaming our finances into the Kingdom of God is the only 100% fail-safe proof type of investment.

Solomon's Wisdom in Sowing & Reaping

Although the principle of Genesis 8:22 concerning sowing and reaping can stand alone, I believe I should briefly expound on the wisdom that Solomon penned as also being foundational concerning the subject from Ecclesiastes 11:1-7 before we move on. I believe there is much we can glean from Solomon seeing that he was one of the wealthiest men that ever lived in the earth. And in that case, let's take a moment to prophetically track through Ecclesiastes 11.

So far, we have previously understood that when verse one of the text talks about casting our bread; it is in context of sowing and reaping according to verses two, four, and six of Ecclesiastes 11. However, in addition to that, the scripture also assures us in verse one that if we cast our bread we will find it again after many days.

In other words, most of the time we don't see results until "after many days" after we've sown. This is the part about sowing and giving that we often don't like to hear. Most would rather treat the offering bucket as a slot machine and automatically hit the jackpot.

However, when we give and sow, we should at least be like Isaac and give the seed at least a year to produce according to Genesis 26:11. We can't treat sowing like the lottery and then get mad at God because we don't get an over-night miracle. Likewise, we can't sporadically and give sporadically and then expect supernatural financial increase.

Ecclesiastes 11:2, 4 is a great reinforcement of this truth. Furthermore, I especially love verse four of the scripture because it teaches us that if we only give when it is convenient for us, we will never learn how to sow and see a harvest. Verse four also teaches that when our harvest comes, it will often be unnoticeable. Therefore, if we are those that are easily discouraged and frustrated in the process of reaping, we will most likely miss our harvest.

Tithing and Giving

Tithing and giving is a lifestyle for my wife and I. I'm so serious about it that I believe that just as people budget their bills, they should also budget their seed, which should be in addition to their tithe. The reason for this is that we cannot afford to give God our leftovers and expect Him to bless it.

My wife and I so believe this that in 2012, during the first year of our marriage, we were sowing at least a thousand-dollar lump sum seed every month for a season, in addition to our tithe and regular offerings. In fact, pertaining to the tithe, I have always only budgeted ninety percent of my money because I understand that ten percent does not belong to me.

I was taught to tithe at a young age, and I am grateful for that, but when I came into the understanding of the tithe and offerings, I began to double my tithe and I also began to sow significantly into the kingdom. I don't double my tithe anymore, but at that time I was tithing in faith for what I wanted to tithe in the future because I had so believed in the principle.

Malachi 3 teaches that we are to prove

God in the area of tithing and giving, and it is the only time in scripture that God said that He would prove Himself to us. God doesn't have to prove anything to anyone because when He makes His appearance it's always undeniable to everyone. However, when it comes to money He insists on proving the point.

In that case, what would happen if more individuals began to tithe prophetically of their desired income? However, that's just a thought, not a doctrine. But if it bears witness with your spirit, I would try it if I were you.

I know many people don't believe in tithing anymore because they say, "we are no longer under the law but under grace". I know in every fiber of my being that this is a trick of the enemy in people's lives, which is why I support the message of tithing wholeheartedly. In fact, there are two simple reasons why I support the message of tithing.

One reason that I support the message of tithing is because if Jesus Himself taught that we ought to tithe in Matthew 23:23, who are we to teach anything different? Jesus is the head of the Church, which is why we should teach what He taught—Old and New Testament included.

And the reason it's important I emphasize that tithing has importance in both the Old and New Testament is because there are many that teach that the Old Testament is no longer relevant because we are no longer under the law, but under grace. For this reason tithing is likewise considered by many as no longer relevant because it was taught in the Old Testament.

However, one of the main problems with the teaching is that it classifies all of the Old Testament under the law, which is error. The truth is that the law was not introduced until a certain point in history in the Old Testament, which is why the Old Testament books are considered to reference both the law and the prophets (Matthew 7:12; 22:40; Luke 24:27,44). In other words, everything in the Old Testament is clearly not considered as being under the law.

Furthermore, when tithing was introduced it was introduced through Abraham hundreds of years prior to the law had ever come into existence. Therefore, the notion that we should do away with tithing because it was under the law is nonsense. Let me explain a little more.

Hebrews 7:1-2 validates tithing as a New Testament principle when it makes reference to when Abraham tithed to Melchizedek in Genesis 14:19-20, and also validates how the order of Melchizedek abides

75

forever according to Hebrews 7:14-17. Furthermore, Melchizedek is key because he is believed to be representative of Jesus in the Old Testament.

In fact, the very blessing of Abraham, that Galatians 3:13-14 teaches that we have received through Jesus, is the very blessing that Abraham received after he tithed to Melchizedek in Genesis 14:19-20. More specifically, the significance of such is that when Abraham tithed, he did so prior to the law, which is why tithing is both an Old and New Testament principle.

Although tithing was included in the law, according to Deuteronomy 26:12, it was in fact in existence prior to the law according Genesis 14:19-20. The difference in the two administrations of tithing is that one tithe was as unto the Lord and the other administration of tithing was under the law.

In other words, when Abraham tithed, he tithed unto the Lord, but under the law, when individuals would tithe, they tithed to the priest. And the big difference between tithing as unto the Lord and tithing under the law is that there was a financial penalty when you missed the tithe under the law, but when you tithe as unto the Lord, you do not merely tithe because you are commanded to, but you tithe because you desire to.

This means that tithing is a matter of the heart. And more specifically, when an individual hears the message of tithing and resists the desire to practice such, it is evidence that there is an issue with the individual's heart that needs to be adjusted. This is why the scriptures teach that where are treasures are, so will our hearts be (Matthew 6:21).

I can go deeper theologically in this, but I won't because it's not the primary focus of my writing. There are many arguments concerning tithing and whether it is necessary in the New Testament that I would rather not explore in greater detail. But one thing for sure is that a man with an argument is always at the mercy to the man with an experience, which is what leads me to the next reason that I support the message of tithing.

The second reason I support the message of tithing and giving is because I have always lived by this and I am a personal witness to its results. The truth is that tithing and offerings mean a whole lot more to a person who counts on it for their very economic survival. I had to learn how to tithe and give because there was no hope for my finances any other way. Maybe the problem is that some individuals feel as if they work hard for what they have and in reality they don't want to give it away because all they've ever expected back from a tithe or offering is a tax write off to begin with.

However, if God was to allow something to bring us to our financial bottom, there would be a lot of people ready to change their theology concerning why they don't tithe. If they ever had to discover—by force—the power of the tithe, they wouldn't care if it were a message of law or grace, old covenant or new covenant. This is a pitfall that I pray everyone reading this book will avoid. I pray that I have learned the hard way so that you can learn the easy way.

Avoiding the Pitfall of Pison

One of the definitions for the root of Pison is "to grow proud". Furthermore, many Jews believe the river Pison is actually associated with pride. So far, in my studies, I believe this pride often surfaces as we work for our money and often forget the difference between money being the source and it being a resource. Therefore, we must remember that there was only one river flowing out of Eden and out of it parted four streams. In other words, God is our source and our career only represents one stream of multiple financial resources.

In fact, working and having a job are two different realities. A job is a "nine-to-five" obligation, but work is connected to purpose and potential. The moment a job becomes our source is the moment we start working under the curse.

However, real wealth comes as we find our purpose and work it. This means that if you are on a job right now, it is only practice for your inheritance. The reason for this is because jobs don't exist to make the employee wealthy, but rather to make the owner wealthy. Therefore, when we understand that our real wealth is coming from another source, it shouldn't be so hard to for us sow what we earn on a job as a seed when God requires it as a means to get us into our purpose.

This giving principle is so important to God that He says if we learn it, He will open the heavens over our lives and give us more than we can handle (Malachi 3). All God asks of us is that we work, tithe, and give on top of the tithe from our hearts, and He will increase what we have. This is what Pison is all about.

We work in order to fulfill God's plan for our lives. We tithe only a tenth out of obedience to remind us that God is our source, and that one hundred percent belongs to Him. Lastly, we give as an expression of faith believing God to bring increase in our lives. If we don't learn this simple principle, we will allow a devourer to steal our increase.

We can't afford to get prideful and begin to think that a job is our source. Jobs come and go. But when you find your purpose, you will never be out of work or out of money. And when you learn to sow your seed, God will never fail to increase you.

At Pison we have to be willing to understand that financial increase involves more than the importance of developing a healthy work ethic. We must more so find the thing we are created to do and work in that specific area. We must also be willing to take seemingly financial risks that involve us channeling our economic resources toward the advancing of God's Kingdom in the earth.

The truth is that we will never live in a wealth zone by merely trying to find a job that pays enough to make ends meet. We are not called to live paycheck to paycheck. God wants to cause us to continually increase, but in order to do so, we must not be afraid to sow and invest while working in the areas that move us towards our destiny. In fact, I don't think it can ever be reiterated enough that we must find our purpose and work it, which leads to our next wealth zone, Gihon.

Chapter 6

Wealth Zone Two- Gihon

Chapter Objectives:
- Learn what Gihon represents
- Understand what has more worth than money in the earth
- Understand that your hidden potential and God given gifts are designed to generate wealth as you cultivate them
- Observe the widow woman's encounter with Elisha, learn from how she overcame financial crisis, and adjust your perspective of economic hardship

The second wealth zone is found in Genesis 2:13, and it is called Gihon. The word Gihon means "to gush forth". Therefore, the revelation is that when this river flows, it is not a gradual increase of finances, but a violent overtaking of blessing.

The scripture teaches that this river compassed the whole land of Ethiopia. The significance of this is that instead of an emphasis on gold, as with Pison, there is rather an emphasis on land that Gihon encompassed.

Furthermore, I believe the emphasis on the land represents natural inherent abilities, talents, and gifting. In other words, this is a wealth zone that you tap into by honing your skills and developing your uniqueness. Gihon teaches us that real value doesn't come from without, but from within.

This is one reason the scripture says we have treasure inside of us. If we understand anything of treasure, we understand that it is something that is to be discovered. Not only is it to be discovered, but also, after being discovered, the value of it is not always immediately recognized or appraised.

As the scripture speaks of the treasure within, I have come to believe that the wealthiest things in the earth are not gold, sliver, diamonds and etc. In fact, the wealthiest people on earth are not the Rothschilds, Rockefeller, and the like. The truth is that the greatest source of wealth in the earth is the power of the Holy Ghost inside of every person that has made Jesus his or her Lord.

What we have inside of us is worth more than money. It is the power within us that raises the dead, heals the sick, and casts out devils. And it is that very same power that gets wealth according to Deuteronomy 8:18.

It's the power of God inside of us that can literally shift economies and cause supernatural multiplication. And if we knew how much we carried inside of us, we would refuse to settle for less. In fact, I prophesy that you will no longer settle for less.

There is treasure within you, and this is the season for you to explore your potential and utilize your strengths. Begin to ask yourself, "What is it that I love to do, or something that I'm naturally good at"? And more specifically, my question to you is, what is it that God has placed inside of you?

In fact, Elisha asked similar questions to a widow woman that was in a financial crisis according to 2 Kings 4. I think we should examine the text and see what we can learn about the revelation of Gihon within it.

Elisha and the Widow Woman

In 2 Kings 4:1-7, I love the story of Elisha and the widow woman who was in debt, because it shows how God can take something that is seemingly insignificant and produce something great out of it. One of the things I love most is that when the widow woman came to the prophet, his response to her was direct, and to the point. The prophet asked the widow, "What shall I do for you and what is in your house?" And in doing so, he both challenged and empowered her.

In fact, the manner in which Elisha questioned the widow woman is a revelation of itself. The reason being is that when Elisha questioned the widow he was challenging her perspective concerning her circumstance to the same extent that he was seeking an answer. In other words, Elisha was trying to cause a paradigm shift in the way that the widow woman looked at her financial hardship.

He was basically saying, "I want to help you, but I have to challenge you in order to do so". Elisha was teaching the widow that the way to escape the financial crisis was to first realize what she already possessed in her house, rather than focus on what she lacked and needed to come into her house. Elisha was teaching her that if she'd only acknowledge what she already possessed, and began to use it, she would have had no problem getting out of the debt that she was faced with.

The revelation is that many times when we are in financial trouble, we are looking towards others to bail us out just as the widow woman was looking towards Elisha. Some have even gone as far as to always look for a handout in life, and because of this, they are missing the economic empowerment that can come about in such moments of financial downturn.

In other words, the truth is that in economic crisis, we are often looking for a solution from a source outside of us when, in actuality, there is nothing that can come into our lives that is more valuable than the things that God has already placed inside of our lives. If we will simply believe that and begin to cultivate the gifts of God inside, we could literally tap into a place of endless supply.

This means that there is a wealth zone called Gihon that is only accessible to those who have the revelation that there is something, designed to bring you economic empowerment, already in your house. Prosperity is already within your house, it is already within your reach, and it is already within you. You were born with God-given talents inside of you that, once cultivated, will attract prosperity.

The issue is that so many people go into careers because it pays the bills. However, there is nothing like getting paid for what you were born to do. But on the contrary, going to school for a well-paying job is often the easy way out. Besides, discovering and developing our God-given potential often takes more time and efforts than many are willing to apply.

By the way, I am not encouraging **that anyone should leave** their current place of employment, or drop out of school. But I am suggesting that you don't get too comfortable where you are at the expense of burying the gifts of God within you. Ultimately, what you must embrace is that at Gihon, your wealth is not in your education, or your career. Your wealth is inside of you.

What is in Your House?

When the prophet asked the widow woman "what is in your house," he not only empowered her but he redirected her focus. In order to answer the question, the widow could no longer focus on her financial problem. She could no longer see herself as a victim of financial crisis.

I'm sure the response of the prophet Elisha was completely different than what she expected. The woman was in need and she was in debt. Yet, the prophet did not come to her rescue, but rather empowered her to see that the help she needed had been within her reach all along.

Consequently, the widow woman was forced do an inventory that led to her financial revolution. In fact, the revolution began for the widow when she informed the prophet of a pot of oil in her home that, to her, seemed irrelevant to her current situation. It was at that point of discovery that the prophet, unlike the widow woman, did not rule out what the widow already had in possession.

Elisha rather gave her an instruction that challenged her to stretch her capacity. He told the widow to go borrow more vessels. And it was in this instruction that everything changed in the widow's finances.

Now let's look at this scenario closely because it just does not make sense. Here is a widow woman in debt, and all she has to her name is a pot of oil. She goes to the prophet for help, and the only solution the prophet has for her is to go borrow more pots, which in actuality puts her in more debt.

There is something we have to understand about the prophet instructing the widow woman to go borrow the vessels. What we must understand is that, at the instruction of the prophet, reality set in and the widow woman realized that God was not intending to snap His fingers and deliver her out of all her financial struggles. God in His wisdom did not merely give the widow woman a miracle, but also a business idea.

And it was from that idea that God was expecting her to begin to work a plan.

Likewise, I reiterate, that if we are going to tap into the next level of wealth, we must be willing to cultivate our ideas, skills, talents, trades and everything else that God has placed within us. This is one reason that Paul told Timothy to stir up the gift that was prophetically imparted into his life (2 Timothy 1:6).

This means that most of the time things are not going to just drop out of heaven on our behalf. Neither can we sit back and wait for someone to come to our financial rescue. We have to know what's in our house, believe in what God has placed inside of us, and put it to work.

Every person reading this book right now is literally full of potential. There is a business idea inside of you, a musical talent, or something else inherent that makes you uniquely different than everyone else. You may have a desire to teach or a gift to write. Whatever it is, you have something to offer the world.

You are innovative and creative. You were born with a unique identity and already posses inside of you everything you need in order to succeed in life—no matter how insignificant you may think it is. When God allowed you to come into this world, He literally placed inside of you an answer and solution to a problem. It is as you cultivate what God has placed within you in order to meet a need that prosperity and wealth will begin to flow in your life.

What is in your house? I pray you take it seriously, because there is a dimension of wealth reserved for those who work what they have. This is why we should have a drive to be the best at who we are and what we do. You are literally priceless.

Blessings of a Lifetime

The last thing, for now at least, that I love about the story of Elisha and the widow woman is the account of what took place after she borrowed the vessels. The reality is that God literally turned her debt into equity. The bible says that as long as she had vessels in her house the oil kept pouring. And not only that, but the widow then sold the vessels that were full of oil, and in doing so, immediately transitioned out of debt into distribution.

The magnitude of this miracle was so large that she literally became an industry leader because of the prophetic word. Likewise, when God finishes with you, and you really tap into Gihon, you will be able to walk off your present job and hire your former boss.

89

Most people do what they can do in order to *keep a job*, but when you tap into Gihon, you do what you love to do and you *offer jobs*. The bible says that the woman sold so much that it brought her whole family out of debt and she lived off of what remained. And the truth is that if you, just as the widow did, will cultivate what is on the inside of your house, there is a wealth zone that you can locate in God that will cause *your oil to keep pouring*.

I prophesy that as you enter into this wealth zone, finances will become cumulative in your life and they will have a residual effect. You are about to tap into the oil that keeps pouring, the gift that keeps giving, and the blessing that keeps blessing. And as you tap into this wealth zone called Gihon, you are not tapping into a season of blessing, but a lifetime of blessing and overflow.

Chapter 7

Wealth Zone Three-Tigris

Chapter Objectives:
- Learn what the Tigris represents
- Learn how revelation can release supernatural wealth
- Learn the 3 Dimensions of financial harvest and how revelation can accelerate harvest
- Learn how you can see an accelerated harvest in your personal life

The third wealth zone is found in Genesis 2:14, and it is called the Tigris River. It is also known as "the Hiddekel". However, the word Tigris literally means "rapid, quick, or sudden". And the emphasis of this wealth zone is not the gold, or the land, but rather the location, which is toward the east of Assyria.

The location of this river is significant in that the east is the direction that the sun rises. Furthermore, the rising of the sun is significant in that it represents revelation. 2 Peter 1:19

talks of how the word is like a light in a dark place that shines until there is a full dawning of the day. The significance of 2 Peter 1:19, in reference to Genesis 2:14, is in how Peter compares the unfolding revelation of God's word with the rising of the sun, which is why I believe this river has an emphasis on revelation.

The truth is that there is supernatural wealth that can come into your life by way of revelation. Isaiah confirms this truth as he mentions the revealing of secret riches hidden in darkness (Isaiah 45:3). Job is another great reference to this as he mentions how he prophetically navigated a vein that led to both silver and a place for gold (Job 28:1).

This will make more sense, as we understand that as Adam lived under the blessing, he didn't live by knowledge but by revelation. This means that this wealth that is coming into your life is coming despite your education, your resume, your qualifications, or etc. It means that people won't be able to rationalize it or figure out how God blessed you financially in the way that He is about to bless you.

Prophetic Announcement

I believe that there is an added apostolic

and prophetic grace coming on the word of faith movement for finances. The world and the devil have fought prosperity preachers so hard because they want to strip the kingdom of its voice. They want the Church to be broke so that it has no influence and no ability to fulfill its mission.

However, this next anointing will be the worse nightmare to all of those who want to endorse poverty in the Church. If they don't like prosperity preachers, it's too late. They are really going to be irritated with the apostles and prophets that God is raising up to preach "good news" to the poor in this coming hour (Luke 4:17).

The truth is that there is an apostolic and prophetic grace that releases an anointing for wealth to flow. It is an anointing that comes by way of revelation, which is why the prophetic anointing is always associated with prosperity according to 2 Chronicles 20:20. This is one thing that the Tigris River represents. It is a wealth zone that you tap into through revelation.

By This Time Tomorrow

Another thing that the Tigris represents by definition is "accelerated harvest". This means that there is a supernatural wealth flow

JONATHAN FERGUSON

that will come by revelation to accelerate the
harvest. When you tap into this wealth zone
there are unusual and rapid wealth
manifestations that will show for it. In fact, CNN
stated in the year of 2012 that America's
economy is slowing down, but those who live in
"The Tigris (rapid; quick; sudden) Zone"
understand that the kingdom of God's economy
only speeds up.

A great example of an accelerated
harvest is found in the life of Elisha in 2 Kings
7:1. The bible records that the nation was in
the midst of a war and in an economic crisis
yet the prophet declares "by this time
tomorrow". He prophesies that the market
would change by the very next day in the midst
of a major recession.

This is significant because if Elisha
could prophesy this under the old covenant,
how much more does it mean, under the new
covenant, that your economic crisis could
literally turn in your favor in just one day.
Twenty- four hours is more than enough time
for God to initiate a wealth transfer.

In fact, in Luke 4:17-19, Jesus spoke of
an anointing to announce the acceptable year
of the Lord. Historically, this was a season
known to the Jews also as the "day" of jubilee.
It is significant because it was during this time
that all debt would be cancelled.

However, this type of economic stimulus would only come about every fifty years, which was the typical time frame of a generation. Therefore, in Luke 4:17-19 Jesus was literally announcing that there is a financial breakthrough that, in times past, only came once every generation, but now could be released every day under the anointing.

God can do in a day what we cannot do in a generation. There is a wealth zone that you can tap into that can release an once-in-a-lifetime type of blessing within twenty- four hours. I believe in over-night miracles because I have seen them take place. I don't teach that everyone always gets over-night miracles, but if and when that anointing is evident, I don't mind claiming them.

The only problem with over-night miracles is that the people who often look for them do not embrace long- term financial responsibility. Despite the controversy, it doesn't take God long to make a wealth transfer. When Israel left Egypt, the wealth of Egypt was literally given to them over-night. Therefore, the reality is that the financial miracle that you have believed for over many years could be released by this time tomorrow.

Accelerated Harvest

We have previously examined how God is obligated to bless His people for as long as the earth exists according to Genesis 8:22, which teaches that as long as the earth remains there will be seedtime and harvest. However, this also means that there is a process of time in between the seed being sown and when the harvest comes forth.

Furthermore, in Mark 4:20, Jesus speaks about the thirty, sixty, and the one hundred fold, which represents three dimensions of harvest. In fact, in order to truly understand Mark 4:20, we have to understand that Jesus is not teaching that some get thirty, others get sixty, and some get one hundred fold. He is rather teaching how the harvest comes in increments. This is why in Mark 4:28, He also talks about the blade, the ear, and the full corn of the crop, which directly correlates to the thirty, sixty, and hundred fold.

In other words, when a seed begins to harvest, the blade comes first, which is thirty fold of the harvest. Next, the ear comes which is the sixty fold. Lastly, the full corn is harvested which is the hundredfold.

The truth is that every seed is designed to produce a hundredfold harvest yet the harvest will come in increments. In fact, any gardener or farmer can tell you harvest doesn't just sprout up all at once. There is a season of sowing and there is a season of harvest, but when you hit this wealth zone the harvest can be accelerated in a very supernatural way.

For example, in Genesis 26:11, the bible says that Isaac had sown seed in bad ground and yet in the same year received one hundredfold. This is significant in that, in the natural, it would have probably taken Isaac at least two years to see these types of results mainly for two reasons. One reason is because the ground would have had to be prepared prior to the seed being sown. The second reason is that the time that it would have taken to both prepare the ground for the seed and afterward allow the seed to grow and harvest would have most likely taken more than a year.

However, I believe Joel had a revelation of this "Isaac-type" of accelerated harvest in Joel 2:23 as he mentions the former and latter rain. This is significant in that the former rain comes to prepare the ground for the seed while the latter rain comes to prepare the ground for the harvest. The former rain was known in Israel as the early or the fall rain and it would come around October or November. The latter rain would be known as the spring rain because it would peak around the springtime. This is significant because the former and latter rain would normally come in two separate seasons yet Joel prophesies not only that the former and latter rain would come, but also that it would come in the same month.

The revelation is that if the former and latter rain would come in the same month, it meant that the harvesters would literally be living in a double season. It meant that there would be a major acceleration in the process of sowing and reaping. It meant that at the same season that individuals would be sowing the seed, they would be also harvesting the seed, which is what Isaac experienced in Genesis 26.

Amos 9:13 also confirms this reality as it teaches that the plowman overtakes the reaper. This literally means that there is such a financial acceleration that before the seed can be sown, the harvest is already showing up.

The Next Dimension of Harvest

I reiterate that there are three dimensions to a financial harvest and release. According to Mark 4:20 there is the thirtyfold, the sixtyfold, and there is the hundredfold. According to Mark 4:28 there is the blade, the ear, and the full corn.

According to Genesis 8:22 there is seed, time, and harvest. However, in this next dimension of harvest, I **prophesy** that time is going to be taken out of the equation and we will go from seed to harvest, and even at times, the harvest will be initiated before the seed is even sown.

The truth is that God wants us to live in a place where we experience prosperity by revelation and accelerated harvest. However, sometimes it's not about the seed you sow, but the revelation you sow into that distinguishes the normal process of harvest versus an accelerated harvest.

In fact, there are some of you reading this book and you feel as if you sow seeds in faith, but you never quite see the manifestation for which you are believing. I am prophesying to you the end of that season.

If you will simply learn to swiftly sow in the seasons and times when revelation is flowing, you will see more swift returns. For example, have you noticed how most churches that preach the prosperity message have taught their followers this important truth?

In churches all across America, individuals no longer wait until a certain time of the service to give an offering, but when they hear the preacher speak revelation that bears witness with their spirits, they automatically bring their offerings and lay them at the altar. In doing so, they have learned how to accelerate their harvest.

When you live in the Tigris wealth zone, there is such a thing as an immediate harvest. This is the type of place in God where as soon as you sow a seed in faith, the miracle you believe for is manifested. When you tap into this wealth zone you longer have to worry if you will ever see the harvest of the seeds you have sown. God literally accelerates your harvest and just as soon as you sow, you are reaping the benefits. May God cause you to begin entering into this **wealth zone in Jesus name.**

Chapter 8

Wealth Zone Four-
The Euphrates River

Chapter Objectives:
- Learn what the Euphrates river represents
- Understand God's commitment to fight for your finances and make the enemy repay you
- Learn how the prophetic anointing is connected to financial deliverance
- Learn of a wealth transfer that took place at the birth of Moses and what it represents
- Understand God's ability and prophetic promise to resurrect your finances

The fourth wealth zone is found in Genesis 2:15 and it is called the Euphrates River. The word Euphrates means fruitfulness, and it is also derived from a word that means, "to break forth and rush".

The Jews associated this "breaking forth" with actually meaning to break out with destructive consequence and results. Therefore, as you enter this wealth zone, not only will you break out of lack, but also there will be destructive consequences for every demon that has been holding your finances hostage.

I'm praying for an anointing to come on you as you complete this book to deal with every harvest eating spirit. I'm declaring that the fruitfulness you should have seen by now, you will see in this next season. There is a prophetic anointing coming into your life much like one of the anointings present in the life of John the Baptist. Let me explain.

A prophet by the name of Kevin Leal gave me great insight concerning one of the reasons why the scriptures teach that John the Baptist would eat locust as his food. The significance is in the fact that locusts are harvest-eating insects. And the revelation is simply that when God sends a prophet into your life, He sends them to eat what's eating your harvest. And I prophesy that there is a prophetic anointing being released in your life to eat up everything that has been eating up your harvest.

Birthing Financial Deliverance

There has always been an undeniable intertwining of the prophetic anointing and great wealth. It was evident in the lives of Abraham, Elijah, Elisha, and other historical prophets. This is one reason why I don't think it could be reiterated enough concerning how the scripture references prosperity to how receptive we are to the prophetic anointing according to 2 Chronicles 20:20. However, I believe that the life of Moses is especially significant in dealing with wealth in a way in which many have overlooked.

In fact, it was through Moses that Israel experienced the wealth transfer that eventually led them into being such a powerful nation. However, although many understand the wealth transfer that took place during Israel's exodus out of Egypt, there is yet another wealth transfer in the life of Moses that I would like to expound on.

I believe there is a revelation of financial release that many fail to acknowledge beginning at the very birth of Moses. Let me show you.

From the time that Moses was born, God had begun to transfer Egypt's wealth. And I believe this took place because of how one of the things that Moses was born to do, as a deliverer, was to bring about financial deliverance. The truth is that Israel's exit out of poverty was just as important as their exit out of Egypt, which is why, likewise with us, God wishes above all things that we prosper to the same extent that our souls prosper (3 John

1:2).

I want you to pay close attention as we see in scripture how, even from his early days, Moses had begun to experience economic release because of the anointing on his life. It is this same type of anointing that is released in this fourth wealth zone, and it will be released in our lives as well. I prophesy that everyone reading this book, and that will ever read this book is about to experience financial deliverance. Now let's get to the point.

Prosperity is a Safeguard

In the book of Exodus, the bible says that when Moses was born, a decree was sent out to kill all the male children (Exodus 1:16). His literal life was under attack. To make a long story short, it was because of this that the bible says that Moses was put in a basket and sat down by a river where the daughter of Pharaoh washed, in hopes of compassion to be shown in order to avoid the death threat of an evil king (Exodus 2:1-6).

However, it wasn't until the Lord began to show me the revelation of wealth zones, in reference to the four rivers of Eden, that it amazed me concerning how Moses was placed in a river in order to escape a death threat. Although I have heard and read the story of Moses plenty of times, it was the revelation of this fourth wealth zone and what it represents that caused this story to come more alive to me. It dawned on me that when Moses landed in this river, he literally hit a wealth zone.

Therefore, when we compare the revelation of the wealth zones with what is recorded of Moses as an infant, it helps us understand why the bible teaches that prosperity is a strong city, or in other words a safety (Proverbs 10:15). In fact, some of you have been under attack and God is saying that you are about to hit a wealth zone that is going to halt the attack against your family, your ministry, your business, or whatever else the enemy has been trying to assassinate in your life. Wealth is about to become your strong city, your safety, and shield you from the attacks of the enemy against your destiny.

What do I mean by this? If you do an inventory of your life, you will notice how the plot of the enemy against your life is nothing more than an attempt to stop you from doing what you are called to do. If you will pay attention, you will notice that most of the struggle in your life is in some way or another connected to some type of financial lack.

This takes place because of how the enemy will always seek to attack your finances in order to kill your destiny while it's in its infant stage. He wants the baby God has given you to die, but the devil is a liar. You can preserve your "Moses" in a wealth zone.

I'm not telling you that money can fix your problems. The truth is that money cannot cast out devils, but it can help get rid of some of the unnecessary problems in your life so that you can focus on the more important things in life. For example, your prayer life shouldn't be distracted because you can't pay your bills.

Your ministry shouldn't have to suffer because individuals are not faithful with their tithes. Whatever your case may be my point is that poverty is the destruction of the poor. This is why the enemy will often monopolize money as a tactic to steal, kill, and destroy purpose, but I prophesy that day to be over (Proverbs 10:15).

In fact, when Moses was found at the river in Exodus 2:1-6, he literally transitioned out of being a slave into living as royalty. This is significant because you may be reading this now, and feel as if, all of your life, all you have known is poverty, but the Lord is saying to you today that you are about to live like royalty. There is a wealth zone in God that can literally change your status from poverty level into an upper class income without years of labor, without inheritance, and without effort. It may not make great theology for some, but you can *take it to the bank*.

A Wealth Zone for Payback

In Exodus 2, not only did the status of Moses change from slave to royalty, but also the bible says that his mother got paid to nurse him (Exodus 2:7-10). This means that Moses not only survives an Old Testament holocaust experience, gets upgraded to royal status, but also his mother literally gets paid in the process. This is so powerful to me because of how the same King that ordered for Moses to be killed ended up paying Moses's mother to keep Moses alive.

For those of you who can receive, I believe God is about to make the devil pay you back for every attack he ever attempted to launch against your destiny and your assignment. The bible says that when the thief is discovered he pays back seven times plus all of the substance of his house. This means that by the mere discovery of this revelation, the enemy owes you—not only what you lost, but also seven times more, and also stuff that never belonged to you (Proverbs 6:31).

I think by now you understand why one of the definitions for this wealth zone means, "to break out with destructive consequence and results". It means that in this wealth zone, you can literally become too expensive for the devil to mess with.

According to Nehemiah 13:2, God is able to turn the curse into a blessing. For example, it was after the life of Moses was threatened that not only he, but also his mother, experienced the greatest blessing of their lives. Let me further explain.

The mother of Moses not only got paid, but she also got paid for doing the thing that I'm sure she loved most, which was being a mother. Can I prophesy? You are about to get paid for enjoying life and doing the thing you love to do most. I will even go as far to tell you that you are literally going to get paid for things that don't even make sense getting paid for. Now if that's not a word, I don't know what is.

Your Finances are Being Resurrected

In conclusion, I want encourage you concerning the purpose of this particular wealth zone. The truth is that you may feel as if you have been in a financial struggle, and if so, that's a good thing. And the reason that it's good is because when the scripture talks about the treasure inside of us, it does so in the context of struggle.

This is significant because wherever there is treasure within, and a struggle without, the bible teaches that it is evident that the life and resurrection power of God is about to be manifested (2 Corinthians 4:7-11). Therefore, it is a good thing, and not a bad thing, that you experienced the struggle and that you experienced the lack, because without such an experience you cannot qualify for this wealth zone.

The truth is that God has you reading this book because He is about to resurrect your finances out of struggle, lack, debt, poverty, divorce, bankruptcy, and etc. God is about to cause this next season to be your most lucrative season and He is about to make the enemy pay you back for all of the affliction that you have had to endure.

So if you are in a struggle, it is good news, because this wealth zone is accompanied with struggle. If you do not believe me, just ask the mother of Moses. She would agree with me that your present suffering is incomparable to the glory that is about to be revealed in your life (Romans 8:18). Oh, and by the way, the first definition of glory in the bible is wealth.

Chapter 9

3 Ways to Get Paid by God

Chapter Objectives:
- Understand the economy and currency system of heaven
- Learn what it means to get paid by God and 3 ways to do so
- Receive a prayer of impartation and never go back to lack and poverty another day in your life

As we conclude our journey together, I want you to understand that Heaven has an economy and currency system. In fact, when Isaiah 55:1 talks about how we can buy without money, it is trying to teach us about heaven's currency and how we can make spiritual exchanges. Understanding wealth zones is about tapping into these types of Kingdom economics.

Therefore, after understanding what wealth zones are, we must also understand that there are some very practical ways of experiencing them. I want to take this last chapter and briefly teach you principles of what I call, *getting paid by God*. In addition to seedtime and harvest, there are other things we can do that will cause us to tap into a supernatural flow of finances. Let's look at the following principles and ask the Lord to help us implement these economic empowerment strategies in our daily lives.

Get Paid in Prayer

What do I mean by getting paid by God? In Hebrews 11:6 the scriptures say that God is a rewarder of them that diligently seek Him. One of the definitions for the word rewarder is "He who pays wages". This means that heaven literally has a pay role and the way you pray— whether it is diligent or not—will determine your pay- check.

Therefore, it is no coincidence that Jesus taught His disciples to pray at least one hour. I believe heaven not only has a pay roll but God pays by the hour. I discuss this principle more in my book *Boot Camp Prayer & The Art of War*. You will need to be sure you get a copy of it or download the eBook for further studies because for now I only want you to understand the basic concept.

My Personal Testimony

If you can work a natural job and get paid a certain hourly rate, what would happen if you start being about Father's business? People often ask me if I am in full-time ministry and my response to them is that I'm in full-time prayer and part-time ministry in order to communicate my seriousness of the task.

I believe that when you are called to full-time ministry you have to be completely devoted to just that. Many sense the call of God, but they can never seem to focus because they are so distracted by money. We have to get to the place in God where we don't worry about how we will provide for our lives and trust God that, as we seek His Kingdom, all of the other things we need in life will be added (Matthew 6:25-33).

The type of commitment that full-time ministry requires often leaves one trying to figure out how they are going to provide for their families. And logic will always want to know how the provision is going to come in our lives. In fact, when I discovered the price I had to pay to truly do the will of God, I wondered how I would fulfill that commitment and make sure finances were flowing at the same time.

But when I found that God pays wages, it revolutionized my life. At the time, I didn't have a job, and I didn't have many preaching engagements. I knew I couldn't compromise my calling and I knew God didn't want me broke. Something had to give.

I then found out that prayer was a way to get paid by God, and that as I took care of His business, He would take care of my business. This revelation helped me not to spend all of my time trying to make ministry connections, study for sermons, and learn offering gimmicks. Instead I spent my hours in prayer, allowed God to divinely connect me, and studied to show myself approved. I found out that as long as I am seeking Him, He keeps me on His pay role.

At that point I began to develop a prayer schedule where I prayed at least seven hours a day as if I was on a full time job. This is what I mean by full-time prayer. You may be reading this, and that sounds like something you will never accomplish, but it's ok because it may be that you don't have the same type of ministry calling.

I was called to ministry, but you may be called to work your business or your career and there is nothing wrong with that. However, if you are called to full-time work, I believe you should at least be engaged in part-time prayer. You may not be called to do what I am doing, but if you begin to seek the Lord diligently in prayer, you too will find that He pays seekers very well.

Prayer is the first way that you get paid by God. Therefore, could it be that there are finances held up in your life because they are not coming from a promotion or a business deal, but they are coming through prayer?

It takes discipline to be on God's pay role, and it is in no way an easy way to success. The process in increasing your pay rate in God is just as demanding as moving up the corporate latter, yet it is very much more rewarding.

I'm not proposing a get-rich-quick idea. There is some discipline involved. In fact, I recommend that anyone in full-time ministry that does not have the capacity to handle four to five hours of prayer daily to do themselves and everyone else a favor in finding another job other than ministry. At the same time, I recommend that everyone—whether you are called to full-time ministry or not—to begin to upgrade your prayer life because you will not be able to tap into any of the wealth zones mentioned in this book apart from prayer.

So stop here and before you continue reading, order my book *Boot Camp Prayer & The Art of War*—you will need it as you continue to advance and grow in your personal prayer life.

Get Paid in Evangelism

Most Christians understand that there are heavenly rewards for those who will do the work of the evangelist and witness to the lost. We understand how we will be rewarded eternally for every person that comes into salvation on our watch. However, Jesus promised us more than an eternal reward for our witness. Jesus taught that when we witness, we not only receive eternal fruit, but also wages according to John 4:36. This is key because, remember, Hebrews 11:6 teaches that God is a rewarder, which is literally defined in the Greek as one who pays wages.

The word "wages" in John 4:36 literally means, "to pay for service". The revelation is that the eternal fruit is what we receive when we get to heaven, yet the wages are what we receive in this life. This is why 1 Timothy 4:8 teaches that godliness has promise for this life and the life to come.

Every time we witness to someone, God pays us. This is why when Jesus sent the disciples out to preach the gospel, they reported that there was nothing that they lacked or needed while doing so (Luke 22:35). Everything in their personal lives was provided for as long as they were committed to advancing the Kingdom of God (Matthew 6:33).

Another great example of this is how Jesus changed Peter's occupation when He called him into ministry. Peter was a fisherman making good money and then Jesus comes along and teaches him how to be a fisher of men. Jesus was basically saying, "Peter, I know you are good at your job in the fishing business, but now I want you to work for me using your fishing skill to rather catch men and bring them into the kingdom".

Therefore, I believe it was no coincidence that when Peter needed money to pay his taxes, Jesus sent him to a fish that had gold in its mouth. It was a very prophetic moment for Peter as the money-miracle sent him a subliminal message, giving him the understanding that as long as he kept working for souls to be saved, as a fisher of men, he would never be without.

If we will likewise commit to being fishers of men we will also discover that God puts His gold in the mouths of fish. This means that God will literally pay you as you evangelize. (Note: Be sure to check out my new book on evangelism entitled *Claiming the World for Jesus*, coming this year: 2014)

Get Paid in Spiritual Warfare

In 1 Corinthians 9:1-14, Paul takes the time to explain how the preacher is called to make his living by preaching. Contrary to popular opinion, this is something that is actually ordained by God. I don't want to go into detail about this because the subject alone is a book in and of itself. However, in verse seven of the text, warfare is mentioned among a list of job descriptions that are compared to the responsibility of the preacher.

In other words, one of the reasons that God ordained preachers to live by preaching is because of the warfare that they have to engage in doing so. It just makes sense. What type of government would expect their soldiers to fight in a war and keep a full-time job at the same time? It just wouldn't make sense and neither does it make sense in the kingdom of God.

1 Corinthians 9:7 teaches that no man goes to war on his own charges or expenses. This is why 2 Timothy 2:2 says that a soldier is not concerned about the cares of life after they are enlisted. The truth is that soldiers are to become government sponsored due to their service in the army so that their focus can be in the battle and not distracted by how they are going to provide for their families. Therefore,

according to scripture, spiritual warfare is one of the job descriptions that God pays preachers to execute.

However, preachers are not the only ones called to war in the Spirit. I believe God is always looking for individuals that He can draft into His army, and it is as we learn the art of war that certain finances are released in our lives.

God promised us that He would give us the treasures of darkness in Isaiah 45:3. He also said that the wealth of the wicked is stored up for the just.

In fact, I believe we overlook a key factor in understanding the wealth transfer. We often overlook the simple fact that the scripture is not merely speaking of the wealth of unsaved individuals, but the wealth of the wicked. In other words, the wealth of the wicked is more so about mob money, drug money, and money that supports other various demonic agendas.

There is money that belongs in the Kingdom of God that is currently being used to fund abortion, sex trafficking, witchcraft, Hollywood's LBGT agendas, and various other social and political corruptions. However, it is only as we learn to war in the Spirit that we can see a release of this type of money.

For example, when Elijah dealt with Ahab and Jezebel the first thing he did was alter the economy as we have previously studied. This was important because Ahab was financially underwriting the witchcraft that Jezebel was practicing. Even Paul, when dealing with the spirit of divination, caused great controversy because of how the deliverance he brought affected the business market and economic status of that city.

The wealth of the wicked is not money that is just simply released and handed over to us. There is a spiritual warfare surrounding this money. In fact, one of the most miraculous wealth transfers in history took place in the midst of a war according to 2 Kings 7.

This is why Jesus taught us that if we will learn how to take the strongman and plunder its stronghold, He would let us enjoy the spoils. This is how we get paid in spiritual warfare. Once a stronghold is pulled down, the finances, that the demonic powers that governed the stronghold were allocating in order to underwrite certain vices in the earth, are then allocated to those who were victorious in bringing the stronghold down.

However, it would be a foolish thing for you to enter into spiritual warfare for the sake of money. Again, I reiterate you will need to purchase my book *Boot Camp Prayer & The Art of War*. It will help you navigate though various protocols that will ensure your safety and victory in the battle.

Fighting for Your Finances

I want to reiterate concerning how I have discovered that most of what charismatic believers label as a demonic attack against their lives is really centered on finances. There is so much depression and demonic oppression that is rooted in money problems. In fact, we have previously examined how the widow woman in 1 Kings 17 is a great example of this. She had become so depressed because of the recession that she had become suicidal.

1 Kings 17 is evidence that the enemy will often attack in the area of depression prior to the biggest blessing in our lives. Therefore, I don't think it is coincident that the rivers flowed out of the garden much like the streams that flow out of the throne and make glad the city of God (Psalm 46:4).

The revelation is that the joy of the Lord is our strength and the enemy knows if he can steal our joy we will, in turn, not have the strength to war. He also knows that if he can touch our finances he can affect our joy.

However, I believe if we begin to war for our finances, there will be such an economic release that we will not only experience a new joy, but even whole cities and governments would begin to submit to our financial counsel and wisdom. Let me explain.

The truth is that we can't even step into a certain level of dominion until we're wealthy because the streams flow in Eden, and Eden is the place where dominion was originally given. Our dominion is directly connected to the blessing.

If you notice in the book of Genesis God blessed man before He gave us dominion. This means that there is no dominion where there is no blessing. It means that if we can't handle money, we can't handle the true authority of the kingdom (Luke 16:9-13).

Therefore, I am convinced that some people that claim to be taking authority over demons and devils are not really taking authority at all. In fact, a person who claims to be effective in spiritual warfare and is broke should not be taken seriously. Even Elijah had to learn how to command the economy before he was able to successfully deal with Jezebel. This is why it amazes me how many people go around "so-called" binding the spirit of Jezebel, but they "choke-up" when its time to command the rain that brings the harvest. Selah.

If we are not going to stand up and begin to fight for our finances, we should likewise stop blaming the devil for many of the things that are coming against our lives and our world. The challenge is however that there are believers, for whatever reason, that enjoy being overly religious about the money issue. Nevertheless, for those of you who are ready to fight for your promise of prosperity, Jesus is ready to cause you to enjoy the spoils as your payment (Matthew 12:29; Mark 3:27).

Conclusion

There are so many different avenues of wealth that God desires you to flow in. He wants to open up the floodgates of heaven and pour out. He wants to favor and increase you beyond what you've ever imagined and this is the season where this is going to become a reality in your life more than ever. There is so much more that can be learned about this subject; however, my assignment was to bring you to this very point of where you place this book down hungry for more.

I pray that this has stirred and inspired you to the place where you will even read again and again until this revelation is imparted into your spirit. I prophesy that any type of spirit of poverty or lack that has attempted to operate in your life has been destroyed. Your mind is now free and liberated to begin to believe God for His highest and His best concerning your finances.

I speak that you are beginning to think like royalty. I say that you will not shy away from greatness, luxury, or wealth. Every religious spirit that may have tried to seduce you on a subconscious level to embrace poverty has exited your life and you are beginning to embrace the goodness of God in your life like never before. There are various wealth zones opening in your life supernaturally even as you read these words, and, most of all, you have it in you to do what it takes to maintain your next dimension of financial increase.

From now on, you will fight victoriously for your finances and you will increase in your giving. You will ever become more effective in the way you witness to the lost, and your prayer life is about to rocket launch. As supernatural increase begins to invade your life, don't ever let the devil trick you and make you think that money is becoming your god. He will attempt to make you feel as if there is something unrighteous about the type of increase that God is about to release in your life. But the devil is a liar.

As long as your desire for prayer is continually increasing and the Father's passion for souls to be saved is burning in your heart, it is literally impossible for money to ever rule over you. As long as you keep these spiritual disciplines in your life strong, the Holy Ghost will keep your motive for money pure and God will continue to give you power to get wealth.

I speak that you are coming out of lack and you will never go back. And finally, I speak that you will always have the provisions and resources necessary to establish God's covenant in the earth, in Jesus name (Deuteronomy 8:18). Amen.

53704485R10070

Made in the USA
Charleston, SC
17 March 2016